Embrace Your Authentic Self

185

Ways

AN EMPOWERMENT GUIDE
FOR WOMEN & GIRLS

Angela Ross

VMH Vikki M. Hankins Publishing
3355 Lenox Rd. NE Suite 750
Atlanta, GA 30326
www.vmhpublishing.com

Printed in the United States of America

10 9 8 7 6 5 4 3 2 1
ISBN: 978-0-9979397-4-3

Cover Design Concept by Angela Ross
Cover Design by Vikki Hankins

Published in the United States an imprint of VMH Vikki M. Hankins Publishing. The publisher is not responsible for websites, social media platforms (or their content) that are not owned by publisher.

To my heartbeat; the reason for my existence - my Grandmother, Salvina Walls. Thank you for teaching me how to be a lady and a strong woman in the midst of abandonment and loneliness. You have been the compass to a sound mind while experiencing failed marriages, sexual and physical abuse, and broken self image.

Thank you for being the light into my world and the living word of God in times when I did not understand and know which way to go

This book is the evidence to the world that what you have taught me has changed my very existence, now it is my turn to teach the young women of the world what you have taught me, self esteem, self worth and valued strength. I said all of this to say, Thank you!

My Grandmother, Salvina Walls

1

I am not a failure.

_____

_____

_____

_____

_____

_____

_____

_____

_____

_____

_____

_____

_____

_____

_____

_____

_____

_____

_____

_____

_____

_____

2

I am accepted.

_____
_____
_____
_____
_____
_____
_____
_____
_____
_____
_____
_____
_____
_____
_____
_____
_____
_____
_____
_____

3

I am awesome.

4

I am ambitious.

_____

_____

_____

_____

_____

_____

_____

_____

_____

_____

_____

_____

_____

_____

_____

_____

_____

_____

_____

_____

5

I am amazing.

_____
_____
_____
_____
_____
_____
_____
_____
_____
_____
_____
_____
_____
_____
_____
_____
_____
_____
_____
_____
_____
_____
_____

6

As you embrace your authentic self you will discover your true fullness!

_____
_____
_____
_____
_____
_____
_____
_____
_____
_____
_____
_____
_____
_____
_____
_____
_____
_____
_____
_____

7

I am aware.

_____
_____
_____
_____
_____
_____
_____
_____
_____
_____
_____
_____
_____
_____
_____
_____
_____
_____
_____
_____
_____
_____
_____
_____
_____

8

I am admired.

9

Do one small thing to make today better than yesterday.

10

I am appreciated.

_____
_____
_____
_____
_____
_____
_____
_____
_____
_____
_____
_____
_____
_____
_____
_____
_____
_____
_____
_____
_____
_____
_____
_____

11

I am adored.

_____
_____
_____
_____
_____
_____
_____
_____
_____
_____
_____
_____
_____
_____
_____
_____
_____
_____
_____
_____
_____
_____
_____
_____
_____

12

I am a good friend.

13

I am a good helper.

_____
_____
_____
_____
_____
_____
_____
_____
_____
_____
_____
_____
_____
_____
_____
_____
_____
_____
_____
_____
_____
_____
_____

14

I am a influence to others.

_____
_____
_____
_____
_____
_____
_____
_____
_____
_____
_____
_____
_____
_____
_____
_____
_____
_____
_____
_____
_____
_____
_____

15

I am a good listener.

16

I am a visionary.

_____
_____
_____
_____
_____
_____
_____
_____
_____
_____
_____
_____
_____
_____
_____
_____
_____
_____
_____
_____
_____
_____

17

I am a great leader.

18

I am a giver.

19

I am a peacemaker.

20

I am able to learn.

_____
_____
_____
_____
_____
_____
_____
_____
_____
_____
_____
_____
_____
_____
_____
_____
_____
_____
_____
_____
_____
_____

21

I am able to share.

22

I am able to love.

_____
_____
_____
_____
_____
_____
_____
_____
_____
_____
_____
_____
_____
_____
_____
_____
_____
_____
_____
_____
_____
_____
_____

23

I am able to assist.

24

I am able to lead.

_____
_____
_____
_____
_____
_____
_____
_____
_____
_____
_____
_____
_____
_____
_____
_____
_____
_____
_____
_____
_____
_____

25

I am authentic.

26

I am brave.

27

I am beautiful.

28

I am bold.

29

I am blessed.

30

I am brilliant.

31

I am bright.

32

Never allow the pain of the process to make you lose your passion for your purpose God has given you! Let your passion for what you do outweigh your frustration from what you do.

_____
_____
_____
_____
_____
_____
_____
_____
_____
_____
_____
_____

33

When we examine ourselves we usually only observe what we want to see. Most of us try to dismiss the truth of who we really are.

_____
_____
_____
_____
_____
_____
_____
_____
_____
_____
_____
_____
_____
_____
_____
_____
_____

34

I will be the best I can be.

_____
_____
_____
_____
_____
_____
_____
_____
_____
_____
_____
_____
_____
_____
_____
_____
_____
_____
_____
_____
_____
_____

35

I am original.

36

I am growing in gratitude.

_____
_____
_____
_____
_____
_____
_____
_____
_____
_____
_____
_____
_____
_____
_____
_____
_____
_____
_____
_____
_____
_____

37

I choose to be happy.

38

I choose to smile.

39

I will love myself.

40

I will believe in me.

_____
_____
_____
_____
_____
_____
_____
_____
_____
_____
_____
_____
_____
_____
_____
_____
_____
_____
_____
_____

41

I will not be negative.

42

I am confident.

43

I am caring.

44

I am a child of worth.

_____
_____
_____
_____
_____
_____
_____
_____
_____
_____
_____
_____
_____
_____
_____
_____
_____
_____
_____
_____
_____

45

I am creative.

46

I am created in the image of God.

_____

_____

_____

_____

_____

_____

_____

_____

_____

_____

_____

_____

_____

_____

_____

_____

_____

_____

_____

47

I am a champion.

48

I will change the world.

_____
_____
_____
_____
_____
_____
_____
_____
_____
_____
_____
_____
_____
_____
_____
_____
_____
_____
_____
_____
_____
_____

49

I am chosen.

50

I am compassionate.

_____
_____
_____
_____
_____
_____
_____
_____
_____
_____
_____
_____
_____
_____
_____
_____
_____
_____
_____
_____
_____

51

I am cherished.

52

I am charming.

53

I am courageous.

54

I am closer to my dreams.

_____
_____
_____
_____
_____
_____
_____
_____
_____
_____
_____
_____
_____
_____
_____
_____
_____
_____
_____
_____
_____

55

I am destined for greatness.

_____
_____
_____
_____
_____
_____
_____
_____
_____
_____
_____
_____
_____
_____
_____
_____
_____
_____
_____
_____
_____
_____
_____
_____

56

I am determined.

57

I am naturally fearless.

58

I am energetic.

59

I am encouraged.

60

I am enough.

61

I am exceptional.

62

I am excited about my future.

_____
_____
_____
_____
_____
_____
_____
_____
_____
_____
_____
_____
_____
_____
_____
_____
_____
_____
_____
_____
_____

63

I am excited about my goals.

_____
_____
_____
_____
_____
_____
_____
_____
_____
_____
_____
_____
_____
_____
_____
_____
_____
_____
_____
_____
_____
_____
_____

64

I can celebrate others.

_____
_____
_____
_____
_____
_____
_____
_____
_____
_____
_____
_____
_____
_____
_____
_____
_____
_____
_____
_____
_____
_____

65

I am fearless.

66

I am fearfully and wonderfully made.

_____

_____

_____

_____

_____

_____

_____

_____

_____

_____

_____

_____

_____

_____

_____

_____

_____

_____

_____

67

I am friendly.

68

I am full of life.

69

I am full of purpose.

_____
_____
_____
_____
_____
_____
_____
_____
_____
_____
_____
_____
_____
_____
_____
_____
_____
_____
_____
_____
_____

70

I am full of joy.

_____
_____
_____
_____
_____
_____
_____
_____
_____
_____
_____
_____
_____
_____
_____
_____
_____
_____
_____
_____
_____

71

I am full of peace.

72

I am full of hope.

_____
_____
_____
_____
_____
_____
_____
_____
_____
_____
_____
_____
_____
_____
_____
_____
_____
_____
_____
_____
_____

73

I am flawed.

74

Authenticity requires us to be compassionate with ourselves, knowing that we will struggle and make mistakes! It requires us to accept life's challenges, and to remember that how we handle those challenges shapes who we are, and who we become.

_____
_____
_____
_____
_____
_____
_____
_____
_____
_____
_____
_____
_____
_____

75

I am God's best.

_____
_____
_____
_____
_____
_____
_____
_____
_____
_____
_____
_____
_____
_____
_____
_____
_____
_____
_____
_____
_____

76

I am God's chosen.

_____
_____
_____
_____
_____
_____
_____
_____
_____
_____
_____
_____
_____
_____
_____
_____
_____
_____
_____
_____
_____
_____
_____

77

I am God's gift.

_____
_____
_____
_____
_____
_____
_____
_____
_____
_____
_____
_____
_____
_____
_____
_____
_____
_____
_____
_____
_____
_____
_____
_____
_____

78

I am confident and determined.

_____
_____
_____
_____
_____
_____
_____
_____
_____
_____
_____
_____
_____
_____
_____
_____
_____
_____

79

I am graceful.

80

I am a girl of purpose.

81

I am a girl of self worth.

82

I am good enough.

83

Being true to yourself is one of the keys to your alignment with authentic happiness.

_____
_____
_____
_____
_____
_____
_____
_____
_____
_____
_____
_____
_____
_____
_____
_____
_____
_____
_____
_____
_____
_____

84

I am at peace.

_____
_____
_____
_____
_____
_____
_____
_____
_____
_____
_____
_____
_____
_____
_____
_____
_____
_____
_____
_____
_____
_____
_____
_____
_____

85

I am healed.

86

I am happy.

87

I am healthy.

88

I am helpful.

_____
_____
_____
_____
_____
_____
_____
_____
_____
_____
_____
_____
_____
_____
_____
_____
_____
_____
_____
_____
_____

89

I am intelligent.

90

I am inspired.

91

I am incredible.

92

I am important.

93

I am joyful.

94

I am thankful for life.

95

I am kind to myself.

96

You can't live your life based on what everyone thinks of you!

_____
_____
_____
_____
_____
_____
_____
_____
_____
_____
_____
_____
_____
_____
_____
_____
_____
_____
_____
_____
_____

97

I can make good choices.

_____
_____
_____
_____
_____
_____
_____
_____
_____
_____
_____
_____
_____
_____
_____
_____
_____
_____
_____
_____
_____
_____
_____
_____
_____

98

So who do you think you are supposed to be? We all have wore a social mask at times.

_____
_____
_____
_____
_____
_____
_____
_____
_____
_____
_____
_____
_____
_____
_____
_____
_____
_____
_____
_____

99

Embracing who you are is a process and it starts with honesty.

_____
_____
_____
_____
_____
_____
_____
_____
_____
_____
_____
_____
_____
_____
_____
_____
_____
_____
_____
_____
_____
_____
_____

100

I am created to love.

_____

_____

_____

_____

_____

_____

_____

_____

_____

_____

_____

_____

_____

_____

_____

_____

_____

_____

_____

_____

101

I am created to give.

102

I am learning everyday.

103

From a very young age, each of us has been asked the question, What do you want to be when you grow up?

_____

_____

_____

_____

_____

_____

_____

_____

_____

_____

_____

_____

_____

_____

_____

_____

_____

104

I am limitless.

105

I am loved by God.

_____
_____
_____
_____
_____
_____
_____
_____
_____
_____
_____
_____
_____
_____
_____
_____
_____
_____
_____
_____
_____
_____

106

I am making a difference.

_____
_____
_____
_____
_____
_____
_____
_____
_____
_____
_____
_____
_____
_____
_____
_____
_____
_____
_____
_____

107

I am me.

108

I am my sister's keeper.

_____
_____
_____
_____
_____
_____
_____
_____
_____
_____
_____
_____
_____
_____
_____
_____
_____
_____
_____
_____
_____

109

I am nice.

_____
_____
_____
_____
_____
_____
_____
_____
_____
_____
_____
_____
_____
_____
_____
_____
_____
_____
_____
_____
_____
_____
_____

110

I am noble.

111

I am not a mistake.

112

I am outstanding.

_____
_____
_____
_____
_____
_____
_____
_____
_____
_____
_____
_____
_____
_____
_____
_____
_____
_____
_____
_____
_____
_____
_____

113

I am one of a kind.

114

I am outgoing.

115

I am pretty.

116

I am a powerhouse.

117

I am pure.

118

I am passionate.

_____
_____
_____
_____
_____
_____
_____
_____
_____
_____
_____
_____
_____
_____
_____
_____
_____
_____
_____
_____

119

I am polite.

120

I am precious.

_____
_____
_____
_____
_____
_____
_____
_____
_____
_____
_____
_____
_____
_____
_____
_____
_____
_____
_____
_____

121

I am proud of myself.

122

I am remarkable.

123

I am a role model.

124

I am respectful.

125

I am responsible.

126

I am somebody special.

_____
_____
_____
_____
_____
_____
_____
_____
_____
_____
_____
_____
_____
_____
_____
_____
_____
_____
_____
_____
_____

127

I am awesome.

128

I am somebody great.

_____
_____
_____
_____
_____
_____
_____
_____
_____
_____
_____
_____
_____
_____
_____
_____
_____
_____
_____
_____
_____
_____
_____

129

I am smart.

130

I am strong.

131

I am sincere.

132

I am successful.

133

I am self confident.

134

I am sensitive.

_____
_____
_____
_____
_____
_____
_____
_____
_____
_____
_____
_____
_____
_____
_____
_____
_____
_____
_____
_____
_____
_____

135

I am somebody of worth.

_____
_____
_____
_____
_____
_____
_____
_____
_____
_____
_____
_____
_____
_____
_____
_____
_____
_____
_____
_____
_____
_____

136

I am someone special.

_____
_____
_____
_____
_____
_____
_____
_____
_____
_____
_____
_____
_____
_____
_____
_____
_____
_____
_____
_____
_____

137

I am wise.

138

I am worthy.

139

I am wealthy.

140

I am a winner.

141

I am wonderful.

142

I am valued.

143

I am victorious.

144

I am visible.

145

I am youthful.

146

I have a beautiful smile.

147

I am talented.

148

I am teachable.

149

I am thankful.

150

I am the best voice of my generation.

151

I am thoughtful.

152

I am unconditionally loved.

153

I am unlimited.

154

I am unique.

155

I am unstoppable.

_____
_____
_____
_____
_____
_____
_____
_____
_____
_____
_____
_____
_____
_____
_____
_____
_____
_____
_____
_____

156

It's important to always show your daughter (s) affection, attention, love, and discipline.

_____
_____
_____
_____
_____
_____
_____
_____
_____
_____
_____
_____
_____
_____
_____
_____
_____
_____
_____
_____

157

Never allow your daughter to feel alone and rejected; oftentimes this can lead to mental illness, identify crises, depression and insecurities.

_____
_____
_____
_____
_____
_____
_____
_____
_____
_____
_____
_____
_____
_____
_____
_____
_____
_____
_____
_____

158

Do you really know who you are?

_____
_____
_____
_____
_____
_____
_____
_____
_____
_____
_____
_____
_____
_____
_____
_____
_____
_____
_____
_____
_____
_____
_____
_____

159

The power of building confidence within you.

_____
_____
_____
_____
_____
_____
_____
_____
_____
_____
_____
_____
_____
_____
_____
_____
_____
_____
_____
_____
_____
_____

160

I am more than my name.

161

Many people struggle with the
question of how to be confident.

_____
_____
_____
_____
_____
_____
_____
_____
_____
_____
_____
_____
_____
_____
_____
_____
_____
_____
_____
_____
_____
_____
_____

162

Think positive thoughts.

163

Remind yourself how worthy you are.

164

Don't give up.

165

I'm imperfectly perfect.

166

Build confidence in your child.

_____
_____
_____
_____
_____
_____
_____
_____
_____
_____
_____
_____
_____
_____
_____
_____
_____
_____
_____
_____
_____
_____

167

You are a collective of every experience in your life, you are how you make others feel.

_____
_____
_____
_____
_____
_____
_____
_____
_____
_____
_____
_____
_____
_____
_____
_____
_____
_____

168

Who are you at your authentic self?

_____
_____
_____
_____
_____
_____
_____
_____
_____
_____
_____
_____
_____
_____
_____
_____
_____
_____
_____
_____
_____

169

Ask yourself what makes you happy, what makes you smile?

170

Our daughters look up to us.

171

Parents have the greatest influence on their children.

172

Show your daughter she is important.

_____
_____
_____
_____
_____
_____
_____
_____
_____
_____
_____
_____
_____
_____
_____
_____
_____
_____
_____
_____
_____
_____

173

Give encouragement and praise them everyday.

_____
_____
_____
_____
_____
_____
_____
_____
_____
_____
_____
_____
_____
_____
_____
_____
_____
_____
_____
_____
_____
_____

174

Give her responsibilities such as chores; girls love to feel important.

175

Spend time with your daughter, don't be so busy.

176

Low self esteem will weigh you down, every stages of life poses its own threats of confidence!

_____
_____
_____
_____
_____
_____
_____
_____
_____
_____
_____
_____
_____
_____
_____
_____
_____
_____
_____

177

Often times with each failure and each mistake we begin to hold all these things inside of us!

_____

_____

_____

_____

_____

_____

_____

_____

_____

_____

_____

_____

_____

_____

_____

_____

178

Stop attacking your self worth.

179

Have you ever just sat and ask yourself who needs me, who cares about me, who am I, will I be accepted, do I have a place in this world or does anybody love me? We have all struggle with this at some point of our life.

_____
_____
_____
_____
_____
_____
_____
_____
_____
_____
_____
_____

180

All children are created worthy.

181

You have to see yourself as unique.

_____
_____
_____
_____
_____
_____
_____
_____
_____
_____
_____
_____
_____
_____
_____
_____
_____
_____
_____
_____
_____
_____
_____

182

Sometimes it can hurt when you have to deal with and admit your inner thoughts.

_____
_____
_____
_____
_____
_____
_____
_____
_____
_____
_____
_____
_____
_____
_____
_____
_____
_____
_____
_____

183

I'm cut from a different cloth. There are no two people in this world that are designed like you. Yes, you may have some similarities, however no one has what you have - your heart, your passion!

_____

_____

_____

_____

_____

_____

_____

_____

_____

_____

_____

_____

_____

_____

_____

_____

184

Never shame, ridicule or compare your child to others.

185

Always talk to and listen to
your child.

_____
_____
_____
_____
_____
_____
_____
_____
_____
_____
_____
_____
_____
_____
_____
_____
_____
_____
_____
_____
_____
_____

To my darling "Pretty Girl" Olivia, if there was no 'you' there would be no purpose for living. You have made my journey into womanhood worth the experience. You are the breath that I breathe, and the thoughts that I think. I would live this same life three times over just to make sure that your future is secure. Thank you for being my joy and my laughter. This book is written for the purpose of young girls like you; that they may find a reason to laugh and the joy in life! love you mom.

Angela Ross and Daughter Olivia

To the women of the world, this book is dedicated to you with the intent that you may realize your true identity! May this book empower you that you may empower someone else!

Everyday think of something positive about yourself and put it in a jar, box or sticky note on your wall for everyday that you read your journal and at the completion of your journey when you begin to have self doubt remember the words you have written down as a daily reminder!

Be Reminded That You Are Beautiful!

About the Author:

Angela is very passionate about our little girls. She desires for them to love themselves as God has created them to be! Her desire is to make sure they know how important they are in the eyes of God!

Her daily prayer is that little girls don't have to experience what she, as well as others, have encountered growing up looking for validation from others. She believes that it is very important to instill encouragement within our girls while they are young. When they get older they will love themselves fully and not grow up with the complex of not being wanted or feeling they are not good enough, pretty enough or smart enough to reach their full potential in their journey ahead.

I appreciate my Honey, Pastor Curtis Ross, Jr. Thank you for your love, support, encouragement and being my pillar of strength. I appreciate you for everything that you do for our children! I adore you! Your wife, Lady Angela Ross "Fancy".

Love Lady Ross

www.ingramcontent.com/pod-product-compliance
Lightning Source LLC
Chambersburg PA
CBHW051056160426
43193CB00010B/1205